How to Draw the Life and Times of
Abraham Lincoln

Roderic Schmidt

LINCOLN ★ DOUGLAS
DEBATE

The Rosen Publishing Group's
PowerKids Press™
New York

To Sarah

Published in 2006 by The Rosen Publishing Group, Inc.
29 East 21st Street, New York, NY 10010

First Edition

Editor: Melissa Acevedo
Layout Design: Julio A. Gil

Illustrations: All illustrations by Ginny Chu.
Photo Credits: pp. 4, 12, 14, 20 (top), 26 (top) Picture History; pp. 7, 24 © Bettmann/Corbis; p. 8
SEF/Art Resource, NY; p. 9 LRC Public Information, Frankfort, KY; p. 10 (top) Rare Book Collection,
Special Collections Research Center, University of Chicago Library; pp. 10 (bottom), 16, 18 Library of
Congress Prints and Photographs Division; p. 20 (bottom) National Portrait Gallery, Smithsonian
Institution/Art Resource, NY; p. 22 (top) © North Carolina Museum of History; p. 22 (bottom) Private
Collection/Bridgeman Art Library; p. 26 (bottom) Library of Congress Rare Book and Special Collections
Division; p. 28 National Archives and Records Administration, Still Picture Unit.

Library of Congress Cataloging-in-Publication Data

Schmidt, Roderic.
How to draw the life and times of Abraham Lincoln / Roderic Schmidt.
    p. cm. — (A kid's guide to drawing the presidents of the United States of America)
Includes bibliographical references and index.
ISBN 1-4042-2993-0 (library binding)
1. Lincoln, Abraham, 1809–1865—Juvenile literature. 2. Presidents—United States—Biography—Juvenile
literature. 3. Drawing—Technique—Juvenile literature. I. Title: Life and times of Abraham Lincoln. II. Title.
III. Series.

E457.905.S355 2006
973.7'092—dc22

2004022498

Manufactured in the United States of America

Contents

From a Log Cabin to the White House

When Abraham Lincoln became the sixteenth U.S. president in 1861, the issue of slavery had already divided the country. Arguments between states that supported slavery and states that did not erupted into the Civil War shortly after Lincoln took office.

The president who tried to bring the United States together during the Civil War came from a humble background. Lincoln was born on February 12, 1809, near Hodgenville, Kentucky, in a log cabin. In 1816, his family moved to Indiana. Lincoln attended school there for a short time but spent most of his days working or reading on his family's farm. In 1831, at the age of 21, Lincoln moved to a town in Illinois called New Salem. He worked at a general store there. Around this time he entered politics. In 1832, Lincoln ran for a seat in the Illinois congress. He lost that race but he ran again in 1834 and won. He served in the Illinois legislature from 1834 to 1842.

In 1836, Lincoln passed his law exam and worked as a lawyer whenever he could find work. In 1846, he was elected to represent Illinois in the U.S. Congress, where he served only one term. By the 1850s, slavery had become a major issue in American politics. Lincoln was against slavery, and in 1854, he spoke out against new laws that would allow slavery to expand. Lincoln quickly became known as the politician who opposed slavery. He ran for the U.S. Senate in 1858, but lost. However, he had attracted attention and in 1860, the Republican Party, whose main goal was to abolish slavery, nominated Lincoln for president.

You will need the following supplies to draw the life and times of Abraham Lincoln:

✓ A sketch pad   ✓ An eraser   ✓ A pencil   ✓ A ruler

These are some of the shapes and drawing terms you need to know:

Horizontal Line	——		Squiggly Line	∿∿
Oval	⬭		Trapezoid	⏢
Rectangle	▭		Triangle	△
Shading			Vertical Line	|
Slanted Line	/		Wavy Line	∿

A Presidency Cut Short

When Abraham Lincoln was elected president on November 6, 1860, Southern states decided to secede from the United States. They believed that Lincoln would end slavery in America. Starting with South Carolina in December 1860, Southern states seceded to form their own country, called the Confederate States of America, or the Confederacy. The states that did not secede were called the Union. By the time Lincoln was sworn in on March 4, 1861, seven states had seceded from the Union. On April 12, 1861, the Confederacy attacked Union-held Fort Sumter in South Carolina, and the Civil War began.

The Emancipation Proclamation was signed in 1863. It made slaves free in the Confederacy and allowed African American men to fight in the Union army. In November 1864, Lincoln was reelected president. On April 9, 1865, the Confederate army surrendered, and the Civil War ended. Sadly Lincoln was assassinated on April 14, 1865, by a man who had wanted the Confederacy to win the Civil War.

This painting, shown in part, is a re-creation of Abraham Lincoln reading the Emancipation Proclamation to his cabinet members on July 22, 1862. It was painted by Francis Carpenter in 1864. The Emancipation Proclamation was first unofficially issued in September 1862.

Lincoln's Youth in Kentucky

Kentucky

Map of the United States of America

This is a re-creation of the log cabin in which Lincoln was born in 1809.

When Kentucky became a state in 1792, Abraham Lincoln's family had already been living there for 10 years. Lincoln was born in a cabin near Hodgenville, Kentucky. In 1811, his family moved to Knob Creek, Kentucky, where they owned a farm. In order for their farm to be successful, the Lincolns had to work hard. The entire family helped plant crops and did various jobs like chopping wood. However, wealthy landowners from other states moved to Kentucky, bringing their African American slaves with them. This caused problems for the people already living in Kentucky. Some needed jobs and the landowners would not hire them. They already had slaves who had to do the work for free. In 1816, when Lincoln's father, Thomas, could not find work after his farm failed, he moved his family to Indiana, where slavery was illegal. Young Lincoln saw what problems slavery could cause for both white and African American people.

The state of Kentucky has found many ways to honor Abraham Lincoln. In 1911, a bronze statue of Lincoln was placed in the center of the Kentucky state capitol, in Frankfort. Lincoln's birthplace near Hodgenville, Kentucky, has been made into a national historic area.

There is a memorial building, a museum, and a reproduction of the log cabin in which Lincoln was born. It is said they used logs that came from his original home. The people of Hodgenville also have a Lincoln festival every year with a parade and an Abraham Lincoln look-alike contest.

This bronze sculpture of Abraham Lincoln was given to the state of Kentucky by J. B. Speed in 1911.

Lincoln Before Politics

As a young boy, Abraham Lincoln had only about one year of formal schooling. He could not go to school regularly because he had to work to help his family. However, Lincoln loved to read and would spend hours reading, as shown in the picture on the bottom right. As he got older, Lincoln took jobs outside the family farm, like working as a ferryman on the nearby Ohio River.

In 1830, the Lincolns moved to Illinois, along the Sangamon River. In 1831, Lincoln was hired to take a flatboat, like the one shown above, filled with goods down the Ohio and Mississippi rivers to New Orleans. During the trip his hatred of slavery grew as he saw slaves being sold and beaten. He also became friends with Denton Offutt, the man who hired him. Offutt offered him a job working at a general store in New Salem, Illinois. Lincoln accepted.

1

The sketch shows one of the flat-bottomed boats that carried goods on the Mississippi and Ohio rivers. Using straight lines draw the body of the boat as shown. Add a short zigzag line to the top of the boat.

2

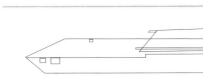

Draw the roof of the boat as shown. When drawing the roof, be careful to leave space between the roof lines and the body of the boat.

3

Using rectangles and lines, add shapes to the roof and to the sides of the boat. Notice how some of the rectangles on the roof stick out past the shapes you drew in step 2.

4

Erase the top parts of the small shapes on the sides of the boat's body and any other extra lines. Draw thin, slanted shapes on the boat's body as shown. Draw four small squares to connect the roof to the boat.

5

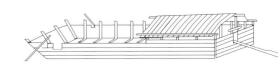

Erase extra lines. Add straight lines between some of the slanted shapes you drew in step 4 to make the floor of the boat. Add slanted lines to the roof of the boat. Draw three oar shapes as shown.

6

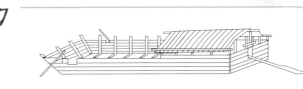

Erase extra lines. Draw horizontal lines along the sides of the boat as shown. Use a ruler or the edge of a paper to make sure your lines are straight and even. The lines on the back are slightly slanted.

7

Add horizontal and slanted lines to the walls inside the boat as shown. Make sure your lines are straight and even.

8

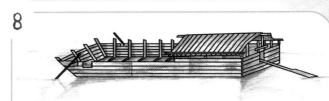

Use the tip of your pencil to shade in the boat and the water. Be sure to shade the inside of the boat darker than the rest of the boat. Your drawing looks perfect!

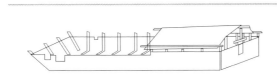

General Stores, Law, and Politics

When Abraham Lincoln returned from his trip to New Orleans in 1831, he moved out of his family's home for the first time and settled in New Salem to

First Berry-Lincoln Store, now U.S. Post Office, New Salem State Park, Lincoln's New Salem, Illinois

work in the new general store. In 1832, he ran for a seat in the Illinois House of Representatives. Of the 300 voters in New Salem, 277 voted for Lincoln. However, he did not get enough votes from other districts so he lost the election. Offutt's store closed shortly afterward. Lincoln then opened his own general store in New Salem, shown above, with the help of a partner, William F. Berry. However, that store also failed. About a year after it opened, the store closed and left Lincoln with no money.

In 1833, Lincoln was appointed postmaster of New Salem, and a year later he decided to run for the Illinois legislature again. This time he won and served for seven years. After Lincoln passed his law exam in 1836, he started working as a lawyer at the law office of John Stuart.

1

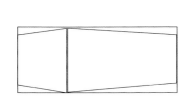

Draw a large rectangle for your guide to Lincoln's general store. Inside the guide draw two sides of the store. Lincoln and his partner William Berry bought the general store in 1833 from the Herndon Brothers.

2

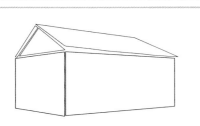

Erase the rectangular guide. Draw the roof using a triangle, a slanted rectangle, and the thin shape as shown. Notice how the roof does not connect to the walls of the store.

3

Draw the shape on the right side of the drawing. Add rectangles for the door and two windows. Draw a chimney. Draw a vertical line in the center of the house's side. Add a slanted line under the roof.

4

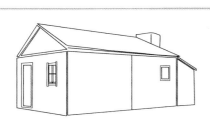

Outline the door and windows using rectangles as shown. Draw connected horizontal and vertical lines in the window on the front of the store.

5

Draw ovals and straight lines along some of the vertical lines of the store. Draw two ovals and curved lines along the edge of the roof as shown. These will be the store's logs.

6

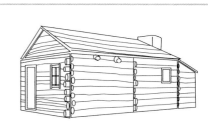

Draw bumpy horizontal lines along the roof and the sides of the store.

7

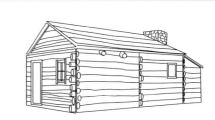

Draw small curved lines on the chimney. These will be the stones.

8

Finish the store by shading and adding shadows on the side. Notice how some parts are darker than others. Add a bush in the back of the store using squiggly lines for the leaves. Great job!

Lincoln in Court

In 1837, a year after passing his law exam, Abraham Lincoln moved to Springfield, Illinois. He met and fell in love with a young woman named Mary Todd. They were married in 1842. Around this time Lincoln began working in the circuit court. This meant that he traveled around Illinois with a team of judges and other lawyers to settle cases for people. He worked all over Illinois, including in the Pekin Courthouse. The picture above shows the desk he used while at Pekin. His experience in the circuit court helped Lincoln build political support for himself because he made many powerful friends in his travels. Often when Lincoln made new friends, he would give them his business card, shown above.

Lincoln had much success as a lawyer because of his talent for public speaking. In 1846, Lincoln ran as a Whig Party candidate for an Illinois seat in the U.S. House of Representatives. He won the election.

1

To draw the desk that Abraham Lincoln used while working at the Pekin Courthouse in Illinois, begin with a slanted rectangle. Add two rectangles on both sides of the first rectangle as shown.

2

Draw a larger slanted rectangle around the the slanted rectangle you drew in step 1. This will be the top part of the desk.

3

Erase the slanted rectangle from step 1. Add lines to the sides of the desktop. Using rectangles, draw two drawers. Add a horizontal line under the top edge of the desk as shown.

4

Erase all extra lines. Add lines to draw the top part of the legs on the right side of the desk. Draw ovals under the top part of the legs. Draw an oval underneath the left drawer.

5

Draw the four legs of the desk as shown. Look carefully at the picture while drawing the legs to see how they get thin at the bottom. Erase any extra lines.

6

Erase extra lines in the legs. Draw a curved line through the top of each leg. Using mostly straight lines, draw the top part of the back of the desk as shown.

7

Erase extra lines. Draw the shapes on the top part of the back of the desk as shown. Add two ovals to the middle of the drawers. These will be the handles.

8

Finish the desk with shading. Some areas are darker than others, so be sure to use the tip of your pencil when shading. Add a shadow on top of the desk as shown. Excellent work!

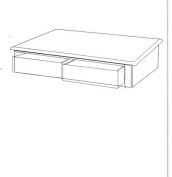

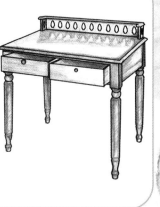

Congressman Lincoln

DU PAGE COUNTY CENTENNIAL

LINCOLN · DOUGLAS DEBATE

AUGUST · 27TH

WEST CHICAGO

After winning a seat in Congress, Abraham Lincoln went to Washington, D.C., the U.S. capital, in 1847. At this time Americans were arguing over the issue of slavery. Lincoln agreed with the Americans who wanted to stop the spread of slavery. Yet he did not think the government should have the power to rid the states of slavery. In 1854, after Lincoln had served his one term in Congress, new laws were created that allowed expansion of slavery in western territories. Lincoln was against these laws. In 1856, he joined the Republican Party to fight against slavery.

In 1858, Lincoln ran for the U.S. Senate against Stephen Douglas. They had live debates on different issues, so the voters would know what each stood for. The debates became famous, as shown by the poster above that advertised a re-creation of the debates performed 81 years later. Lincoln lost the election, but his popularity increased. In 1860, the Republican Party nominated him to run for U.S. president.

1

The Lincoln-Douglas debates were re-created in 1939 at the 100-year celebration of the founding of DuPage County. Begin the picture on the poster by drawing a circle.

2

Draw a bigger circle around the circle from step 1. Add a larger circle around the two circles as shown. Draw four stars inside the larger circle as shown. Add a star on either side of the large circle.

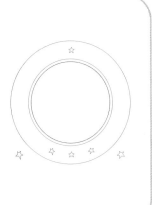

3

Inside the larger circle, add the word "LINCOLN" on the left side. The word will be between the top star and the bottom star on the left.

4

On the right side of the larger circle, write "DOUGLAS." The word will be between the top star and the bottom star on the right. Add a larger circle as shown for a guide.

5

Use the circle from step 4 to write the word "DEBATE" between the two stars on the bottom. Draw the shapes for the heads of Lincoln and Douglas inside the center circle as shown.

6

Erase the circle from step 4. Begin to draw the faces and hair of Lincoln and Douglas as shown using squiggly lines.

7

Finish drawing the squiggly lines on their heads. Add lines to their necks and shoulders as shown.

8

Finish your drawing by shading in the words and the rest of the picture using the tip of your pencil. Notice how some parts are darker than others. Great work!

President Lincoln and the Start of the Civil War

Abraham Lincoln won the presidency on November 6, 1860. Knowing his opinion of slavery, many Southern states thought he would abolish slavery. By March

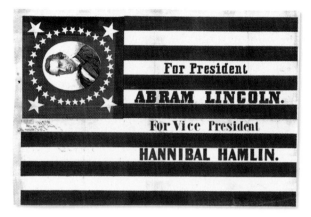

1861, when Lincoln took office, seven Southern states had seceded from the United States to form their own country, called the Confederacy. Lincoln tried to get them to return to the United States, or the Union. His efforts failed and on April 12, 1861, Confederate soldiers attacked Fort Sumter, a Union-held fort in South Carolina's harbor. This was the start of the Civil War.

Lincoln knew that the United States could not exist if the country was divided over slavery. He decided that fighting against slavery was the only way to save the Union. As the war went on, four more Southern states joined the Confederacy in the summer of 1861. Even though the Union had more money to put into the war, the Confederate army had more experienced generals and won many of the early battles.

1

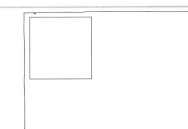

This banner was used during Lincoln's campaign for president in 1860. Draw a large rectangle. Inside the rectangle draw a big square in the upper left corner as shown.

2

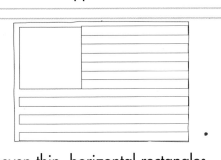

Draw seven thin, horizontal rectangles across the body of the banner. Use a ruler to make straight, even lines. You will have 13 stripes.

3

Inside the center of the square, draw an oval. Add small stars around the oval as shown. Draw four larger stars in each corner of the square.

4

Write "FOR PRESIDENT" in the fourth stripe from the top. Begin drawing the guides for Lincoln with a small oval in the large oval. Add lines as shown. Lincoln will be sideways.

5

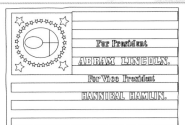

Add the rest of the words, skipping a space between each. Write "ABRAM LINCOLN." Then write "FOR VICE PRESIDENT." Lastly write "HANNIBAL HAMLIN."

6

Using curved lines, draw Lincoln's shoulders and clothes. Draw in his hair using a squiggly line. Add three horizontal lines in the oval for guides for the eyes, nose, and mouth.

7

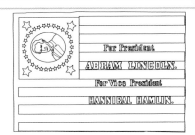

Erase the guides. Using the face guides, draw in his eyes, nose, and mouth. Add details to Lincoln's ear. Add lines to his collar.

8

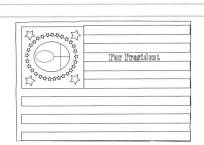

Erase extra lines. Finish the banner by shading. Notice how some parts of the banner are darker than others. Fill in the letters. What a great job!

19

The Emancipation Proclamation

Soon after the Civil War started, Abraham Lincoln saw that the only way to save the Union was to rid the entire country of slavery. He still did not believe that the government had the power to do this, so accomplishing it was tricky.

Lincoln encouraged the few slave states in the Union to end slavery on their own. When this failed, he issued the Preliminary Emancipation Proclamation on September 22, 1862. The proclamation stated that if the Confederacy did not surrender within 100 days, the Union would set all of their slaves free. When the Confederacy did not surrender, Lincoln signed the final Emancipation Proclamation using the pen shown above, on January 1, 1863. The proclamation, shown above in the bottom picture, said the slaves in the Confederacy were free and welcome to join the Union army.

1

The gold pen Lincoln used to sign the Emancipation Proclamation on January 1, 1863, still has its original leather-covered box. Begin the case by drawing a rectangle.

2

Use a ruler or the edge of your paper to draw two slanted rectangular shapes inside the rectangle as shown.

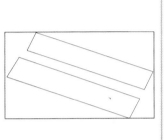

3

Erase the rectangular guide. Draw an outline of the pen's case around the rectangular shapes you drew in step 2 as shown.

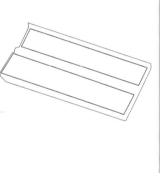

4

Draw a slightly larger rectangular shape around the top shape. Draw a shape inside the bottom rectangular shape as shown.

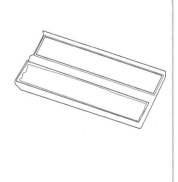

5

Using squiggly lines, decorate the edges of the pen case as shown.

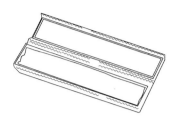

6

Draw the shape for the pen as shown. Notice how the pen is positioned against the case at a vertical angle. Also note how thin the pen gets toward the bottom.

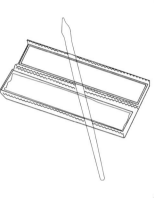

7

Erase any extra lines. Draw four slightly curved lines on the pen for the details.

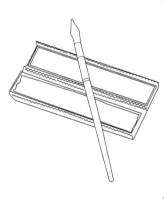

8

Finish your drawing by shading in the case with the side of your pencil. Notice how some areas are darker than others. Great work!

The Battle of Gettysburg

Most of the Civil War's battles had taken place in Confederate territory. Robert E. Lee, a Confederate general, decided to attack Union territory. On July 1, 1863, Lee's army met General George Meade's Union army in Gettysburg, Pennsylvania. They fought for three days. About 51,000

men were killed or wounded. The bottom painting above shows the battle. The Confederate army was forced to retreat. Their flag is shown above at the top.

On November 19, 1863, Abraham Lincoln dedicated a new national graveyard in Gettysburg to honor all the men who had died there. He gave a famous speech, known as the Gettysburg Address, in which he reminded Americans that all men are equal and that they needed to fight for freedom.

1

To draw the Confederate flag, begin with a rectangle.

2

Draw a squiggly shape inside the rectangle as shown.

3

Erase the rectangle from step 1. Draw a vertical line on the left side of the flag. Draw two lines to make a square in the upper left corner of the flag. Draw an *X* inside the square.

4

Outline the *X* in the square as shown. Add a short line to the bottom of the flag on the left.

5

Erase the center part of the *X* in the square. Add stars in the *X* as shown.

6

Add the rest of the stars on the *X*.

7

Finish the Confederate flag by shading. The flag is old, so you can add holes and tears on the flag. Great work!

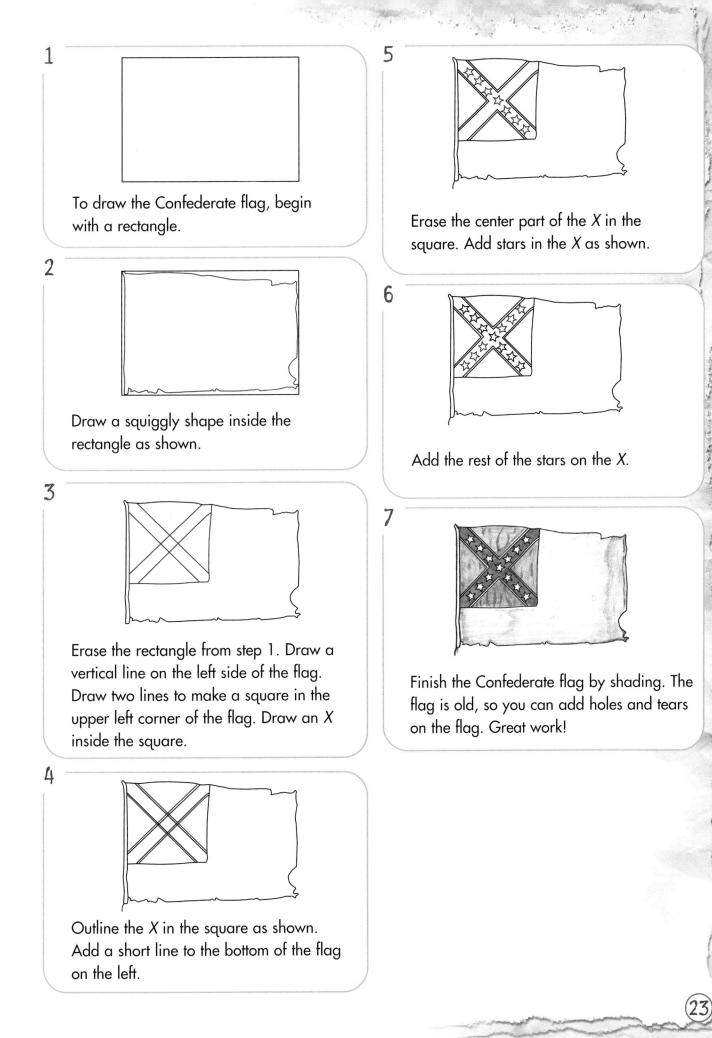

The End of the Civil War

After the Battle of Gettysburg, President Abraham Lincoln did his best to win the war. In 1864, he made General Ulysses S. Grant commander of the Union army. Grant had fought several battles against Confederate troops. In addition to being concerned

about the war, Lincoln worried about being reelected in 1864. Some people did not agree with how Lincoln was managing the war. It was possible that he could lose the election. Fortunately, Union armies won a series of battles shortly before the election. On November 8, 1864, Lincoln was reelected. The medal above is from the 1864 campaign.

On April 3, 1865, Union forces captured Richmond, Virginia, the capital of the Confederacy. On April 9, 1865, the last large Confederate army surrendered to General Grant in Virginia. The Civil War was over, and the Union had won.

1

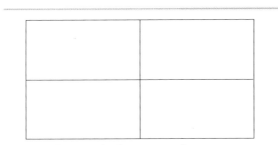

To draw the eagle from Lincoln's 1864 campaign medal, start with a large rectangle. Draw a horizontal line and a vertical line that cross at the middle.

2

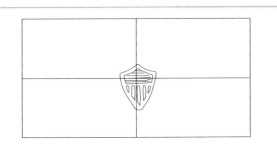

Draw a shield in the center of the rectangle as shown. Add shapes and lines to the inside of the shield.

3

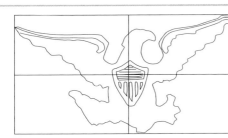

Draw an outline of the eagle inside the rectangle as shown. Notice how his wings are shaped and the extra lines that make up his wings on the top.

4

Erase the guides. Using lines draw feathers on the left wing of the eagle. Draw the face of the eagle using squiggly lines.

5

Draw the feathers on the right wing of the eagle as shown.

6

Add the leaves to the bottom part of the eagle using curved and slanted lines as shown. Draw the legs and claws of the eagle using squiggly lines.

7

Draw the arrows that the eagle is holding in its right claw. Using squiggly lines add the rest of the details to the legs.

8

Finish the drawing of the eagle by shading with the tip of your pencil. Notice how some areas are darker than others. Excellent work!

Lincoln Is Assassinated

Many Americans had mixed feelings at the end of the Civil War. Some viewed Abraham Lincoln as a hero. Others wanted slavery to continue and hated Lincoln for the war they believed he had caused. John Wilkes Booth was one of those people. Before the end of the war, Booth had planned to kidnap Lincoln to force him to return the Confederate prisoners of war. When the Civil War ended two weeks later, Booth decided to kill Lincoln instead.

On April 14, 1865, just five days after the end of the war, Lincoln went to Ford's Theatre in Washington, D.C., to see a play. Booth snuck into the theatre and shot Lincoln in the head as he sat in the rocking chair pictured at the top. Lincoln died the next day on April 15, 1865. The painting above shows Lincoln's assassination.

1 Draw a large square to start the chair in which Lincoln sat when he was shot. Draw a horizontal line across the bottom. Draw the shapes above and below the line as shown.

2 To create the back of the chair, draw curvy lines inside the slanted rectangle on top of the horizontal line. Draw a curvy line inside the shape on the bottom of the line to create the seat cushion.

3 Erase the square, the horizontal line, and the top guide for the chair. Add the arms of the chair with arm cushions as shown. Use squiggly lines to create the details on the arms.

4 Erase the guide for the seat bottom and any extra lines. Add the bottom of the chair under the seat cushion as shown. Begin the back leg.

5 Draw the two legs on the left side of the chair. Draw a curve for the bottom part of the chair.

6 Draw the other two legs on the right side of the chair. Draw another curve like the one you drew in step 5 on the right side.

7 Add small circles on the back of the chair as shown. Draw lines from the center of the circles outward. Add lines to the cushion and the chair's frame as shown.

8 Finish with detailed shading. Add light shadows to the cushions. Your chair looks great!

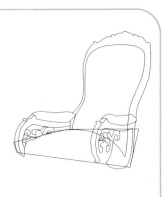

The Great Emancipator

Abraham Lincoln is considered to be one of the greatest presidents of the United States. He led the country through the Civil War, one of the most challenging times in history. When his family was not wealthy enough to send him to school, he worked hard to educate himself. He  was moral and honest. Early in his life, he realized how horrible slavery was, and he spent most of his adult life fighting for freedom for all people. Lincoln was also very wise, and he knew that he could not use the federal government to abolish slavery without the help of the people. He worked hard to convince the people that slavery was wrong. While the Emancipation Proclamation was a great start, he continued to work on abolishing slavery by getting the Thirteenth Amendment to the U.S. Constitution ratified on December 6, 1865. The Thirteenth Amendment ended slavery in the United States forever. For his efforts in securing freedom for all, Abraham Lincoln will always be known as the Great Emancipator.

1

To draw the picture of Abraham Lincoln taken by Mathew Brady, start with a large rectangle. Add lines. Add an oval and a curved line for the head. Draw an oval for the ear.

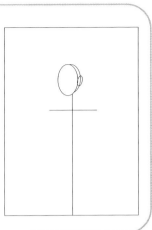

2

Draw three small horizontal lines in the oval. These will be guides for the face. Add curvy lines for the shoulders and arms as shown.

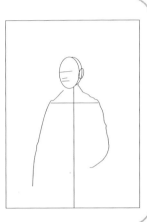

3

Erase part of the head oval. Add lines for the collar and edge of the jacket. Add a line for a sleeve. Erase the horizontal body line. Add an oval on the left side for a sleeve opening.

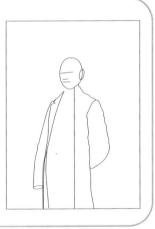

4

Erase the straight vertical line and any extra lines. Draw the collar and edge of the jacket on the right side. Draw the bow tie and a *V* for the vest. Draw the beard and outline of his face.

5

Erase the bottom of the ear guide. Using the guides, add ovals for the eyes. Draw the nose and the mouth. Add eyebrows and a line by the ear. Draw the pants and the hand.

6

Erase extra lines. Use a squiggly line to create the hair. Add lines to his face. Add lines to his ear. Draw more hair below the ear, too.

7

Add a slanted line in front of his shirt as shown. This is his vest. Draw circles down the right side for his vest buttons. Add four circles on the outside of the jacket. Add lines to his eyes and ear.

8

Finish Lincoln by shading. Shade in the hair, the vest, his left shoulder, and the left side of his face darker than the rest of him. You are finished. Good work!

Timeline

1809 On February 12, Abraham Lincoln is born to Thomas and Nancy Lincoln near Hodgenville, Kentucky.

1811 The Lincoln family moves about 15 miles (24 km) to a farm in Knob Creek, Kentucky.

1831 Abraham Lincoln is hired to pilot a flatboat down the Ohio and Mississippi rivers to New Orleans.

1834 Lincoln successfully runs for the Illinois House of Representatives. He will be reelected in 1836, 1838, and 1840.

1836 Lincoln passes his law exam and joins John Stuart's law office.

1842 Lincoln marries Mary Todd.

1846 Lincoln is elected to represent Illinois in the U.S. House of Representatives.

1854 On July 6, the Republican Party is formed in Jackson, Michigan. The party is made up of people who all oppose the expansion of slavery.

1858 From August 21 to October 15, Lincoln has a series of debates with Stephen Douglas as they compete for one of Illinois's seats in the U.S. Senate. Lincoln becomes well known for his antislavery speeches.

1860 On May 18, Lincoln wins the Republican nomination for president, and on November 6, Lincoln is elected president.

1861 On March 4, Lincoln is sworn in as president.

On April 12, Confederate forces attack Union-held Fort Sumter, which starts the Civil War.

1863 Lincoln issues the final Emancipation Proclamation, which frees slaves in the rebellious states.

The Battle of Gettysburg is fought.

1864 November 8, Lincoln is reelected president.

1865 On April 9, the Confederate army, under General Robert E. Lee, surrenders. The Civil War ends.

April 14, Lincoln is shot by John Wilkes Booth in Ford's Theatre in Washington, D.C., and dies early the next morning.

Glossary

abolish (uh-BAH-lish) To do away with.

amendment (uh-MEND-ment) An addition or a change to the Constitution.

assassinated (uh-SA-sih-nayt-ed) Killed suddenly.

candidate (KAN-dih-dayt) A person who runs in an election.

Civil War (SIH-vul WOR) The war fought between the Northern and Southern states of America from 1861 to 1865.

Confederacy (kun-FEH-duh-reh-see) The 11 Southern states that proclaimed themselves separate from the United States in 1860 and 1861.

debates (dih-BAYTS) Arguments or discussions.

dedicated (DEH-dih-kayt-ed) To have given to a purpose.

Emancipation Proclamation (ih-man-sih-PAY-shun prah-kluh-MAY-shun) A paper, signed by Lincoln during the Civil War, that freed all slaves held in Southern territory.

expansion (ek-SPAN-shun) The widening or opening of an area.

kidnap (KID-nap) To carry off a person by force.

lawyer (LOY-er) A person who gives advice about the law and who speaks for people in court.

legislature (LEH-jis-lay-chur) A body of people that has the power to make or pass laws.

medal (MEH-dul) A small piece of metal that is given to honor someone.

nominated (NAH-mih-nayt-ed) To have suggested that someone or something should be given an award or a position.

partner (PART-ner) A person with whom someone works.

ratified (RA-tih-fyd) Approved or agreed to something in an official way.

Republican Party (rih-PUH-blih-ken) One of the two major political parties in the United States.

secede (sih-SEED) To withdraw from a group or a country.

surrendered (suh-REN-derd) Gave up.

Union (YOON-yun) The Northern states that stayed with the federal government during the Civil War.

Whig Party (WIG PAR-tee) A political party formed in 1834 in opposition to the Democratic Party.

Index

Web Sites

Due to the changing nature of Internet links, PowerKids Press has developed an online list of Web sites related to the subject of this book. This site is updated regularly. Please use this link to access the list:
www.powerkidslinks.com/kgdpusa/lincoln/

32